NOT to Say

Dedicated to—
Justin and Missy Cannon
Neighbors who define friendship through action

David and Janet Clifton
Who exemplify the best in humanity

Call Me If You Need Anything… and Other Things NOT to Say

A Guide to Helping Others through Tragedy and Grief

CATHY PETERSON

CHALICE
PRESS

ST. LOUIS, MISSOURI

Cover art: FotoSearch
Cover and interior design: Elizabeth Wright

This book is printed on acid-free, recycled paper.

Visit Chalice Press on the World Wide Web at
www.chalicepress.com

10 9 8 7 6 5 4 3 2 1   05 06 07 08 09

Library of Congress Cataloging–in–Publication Data
Peterson, Cathy (Cathy A.)
  Call me if you need anything and other things not to say :
a guide to helping others through tragedy and grief / Cathy
Peterson.
      p. cm.
  ISBN 13: 978-0-827204-98-1 (pbk. : alk. paper)
  ISBN 10: 0-827204-98-1
  1. Church work with the terminally ill. 2. Church work
with the bereaved. I. Title.
  BV4460.6.P48 2005
  259'.6—dc22
                                          2004025378

Printed in the United States of America

Contents

Preface

There are rare times in life when one encounters someone going through severe trials or difficulties with unique courage and determination. Cathy Peterson is such a person. Not only has she faced some of the toughest things life has to offer, but with God's strength, she has demonstrated a heart to help others.

All of us at one time or another have sincerely wondered what to do or say to help someone going through a difficult situation. Or we have personally gone through our own crisis and wished people instinctively knew how to help.

Cathy Peterson, having gone through her own time of great suffering and loss, gives us some very personal and practical insights into helping others. As the apostle Paul wrote in 1 Corinthians 12:26a, "If one member suffers, all the members suffer with it..."

Jere A. Wilson, pastor,
First Baptist Church
Henderson, Texas

The Fog

Need # 1

Time alone—about three to four days

The news was not good. It was cancer. My middle-aged husband was facing the fight of his life. Our immediate response was shock. Our first impulse, our first emotional need, our primal *necessity* was time alone—a time of solace to absorb the news and attempt to escape the fog that seemed to suffocate our very being.

The fog emerged almost immediately and trapped our intellect, reasoning and even our emotions in what seemed like a thick, white murkiness that was inescapable.

It felt as if we were driving down an unfamiliar road on a dark, cold night, straining to find our way, shrouded by thick smog. The situation controlled us as surely as if we were its captives.

Slowly, ever-so-slowly, the fog seemed to lift and then reappear.

As a friend to a befogged person, initially give the family the gift of time. Don't besiege them with telephone calls or visits asking questions and/or giving advice. Allow them "absorption time."

If you are a close friend, you might volunteer to serve as the family's "coordinator" in sharing initial medical information with friends and in serving as the contact person for those bringing meals. Concerned friends can contact the coordinator and learn of needs they can pray about or physically assist with.

An example would be Renee, a dear friend whose husband was recently diagnosed with a brain tumor. Upon returning home from a long day at the hospital, she found her kitchen floor flooded! Within minutes, she discovered a broken icemaker water line. The coordinator learned of the incident and arranged to meet a plumber the next day.

In addition, Renee's friends called the coordinator to arrange the gift of meals. This reduced confusion and the problem of having too much or not enough food, prevented the giver from taking the same meal (like roast or spaghetti) as another, and created clarity about the number of persons to be fed.

The coordinator would then make one call to Renee and advise her of the delivery schedule. Friends liked the efficiency of having a coordinator because they felt they could call anytime for an update and that the needs of the patient and family were being met.

Many times, the family is advised to "get business affairs in order" before treatment begins. Spiritual, financial, and attitude decisions must be made to positively steer into the future.

Sitting at the kitchen table the morning after the diagnosis, my husband and I agreed that bitterness was not an option. Years earlier, we knew a couple who had lost their only child in a car accident. We watched as their grief turned to anger and anger into bitterness and bitterness into progressively caustic behavior. Months turned into years, and their corrosive spirit alienated friends, family, God-sent opportunities, and the ability to enjoy even the simplest joys. We learned that the price of bitterness was too high, and we vowed not to pay it, no matter the challenges we faced.

For several days, our next door neighbors, Sam and Ghada, brought a small meal each evening. Our appetites were small—food didn't seem a priority. What did she do to entice us? Cleverly, she prepared all our favorite dishes! Her acts of kindness ministered to our hearts and strengthened us physically for the days ahead.

Preparing for treatment can be compared somewhat to going to school for the first time. You feel overwhelmed, scared, and you're not sure if you're big enough to go! Just like school supplies, you need hospital supplies. These supplies make wonderful and practical gifts.

The first thing you might give is a spiral notebook or three-ring binder with a pen. Section the notebook! Make the first section for important phone and cell numbers. The second section is for notes. The caregiver uses this section for information the physician shares. This sounds unnecessary, but fatigue quickly robs clarity. The notes become invaluable in remembering what the doctor said. The third section is for a daily diary. This historical information tracks treatment and reactions. It serves as a road map in anticipating symptoms in subsequent treatments or hospitalizations.

A calendar is a priority. Treatments, appointments, and hospitalizations are posted for personal organization. Without a calendar, and more quickly than you can imagine, the family will be asking, "What day of the week is it?"

Like an apple for the teacher, candy is a must—for the nurses! The gift of candy gives the patient an opportunity to show appreciation without the extra expense. Give a large plastic bowl and bags of individually wrapped candy. This small gift will bring smiles to both the nurses and the patient.

Days pass, and like a haze that disappears with the warmth of the sun, the haze lifts from the mind. The time of absorption is over—reality is as clear as mid-morning.

The first immediate need is time alone—about three to four days.

2

Facing the Road Ahead

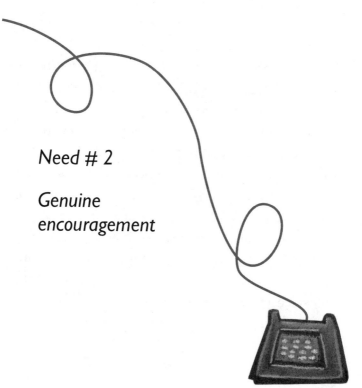

Need # 2

*Genuine
encouragement*

We then experienced a sense of clarity and a firm resolution to face the adversity head-on. This is the time for active encouragement from friends and family.

Cards in the mailbox are like bottled water to a runner on a marathon. Send cards that share messages of "overcoming obstacles," and "we believe in you," cards with scripture promises, and/or better yet, cards with hilarious messages. Send a St Patrick's Day or Christmas card at the opposite time of year and say, "I thought you might be tired of getting the same old cards—just thinking of you." It's guaranteed to bring a laugh and lift the spirits—for the whole family! Send a card once a week or even more often—it's impossible to share too much encouragement!

We received a Thanksgiving card in July from a friend known for his positive spirit. He crossed out the message and wrote that it was the only card he had! It brought instant laughter and lifted our spirits for an entire day!

Remember that many times a recently diagnosed cancer patient doesn't *feel* sick. A get-well card doesn't seem relevant. Incidentally, if the prognosis is very poor, do not send a get-well card. This well-intended card can bring despondency to the recipient and to the family.

An option would be to purchase a greeting card software program and design your own personal cards using the patient's name. Send funny anonymous cards, allowing the patient to wonder which of his many friends is sending this. The fun is in the guessing!

Cards like "Joe—Your hospital gown gave I.C.U. an entirely different meaning!" or a card with a beautiful woman on front with the words inside, "Joe… check your pulse—I'm going to be your nurse!" Use your imagination, and create fun for the patient! Your card may be the brightest spot of the day! He can read and reread your card, share it with friends, and feel the caring over and over.

Make phone calls brief, and be available to *listen*. Initially the family has little medical information and won't have a lot of details to share. They're on a path they may never have traveled before—fear and uncertainty are their traveling companions.

Don't share bad experiences that have happened to someone you know. Use the adage, "If you don't have anything nice to say, don't say anything at all." Don't be the "hospital buzzard" flying around with negativity. In fact, if you have a hospital buzzard around your loved one, encourage him or her not to visit.

Don't call unless you are sincere. This may sound odd, but just as some motorists slow down to see an auto accident out of curiosity, some folks call for the same reason. The person receiving this kind of call quickly senses the intent and feels exploited.

When you call, don't *offer* to help. Make an action plan to help. Don't *offer* to mow the grass. Say, "I'm coming over Friday evening to mow your grass," or simply give a "surprise mow." Common sense will lead you to know what needs *you would experience* in the same situation. Follow your heart, and *act*.

Listening is *key* in any telephone or personal conversation. What unique need do you perceive that the patient or family has?

Treatment in our case occurred during the summer. Our backyard served as our tropical paradise and refuge, yet watering the yard and numerous potted plants became a challenge. One afternoon, I shared with a friend that I was leaving the hospital early to water plants. *Listening*, she quickly offered to do it on a regular basis—allowing me freedom from that responsibility and anxiety. Her gift of time—and that of others—encouraged us to "fight the good fight."

The second need is genuine encouragement.

3

Roadblocks

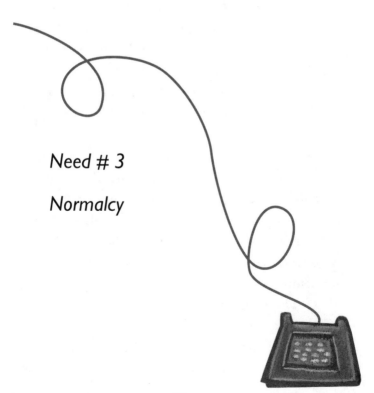

Need # 3

Normalcy

The word is now out to your neighbors, friends, acquaintances, and coworkers. You have a serious illness.

This is one of the most challenging aspects of a serious illness—people's reactions. The most prominent reaction we found was avoidance. Neighbors initially raced into their homes with an embarrassing nod. Invitations for get-togethers stopped. Friends stopped dropping in. Water-cooler chitchat at the office ceased.

Why? People didn't know what to say.

What did we want? Normalcy. We wanted our life to continue as before the diagnosis. We were still capable of laughing, having a good time, socializing, and even eating! In fact, we *needed* social interaction to maintain a positive mental outlook. In reality, we were *exactly* the same people except for the challenge set before us.

Our best source of normalcy was my twin sister and brother-in-law. Cancer was forgotten, and we interacted instinctively like we had for years. We were still "us," and they were still "them." My brother-in-law affectionately nicknamed my husband, "Lucky," and it was medicinal! They turned the challenges into laughter, and together they acknowledged the situation as "the pits." It was medicinal to know that someone understood.

Invitations provide a positive and refreshing diversion to the patient. Be flexible. The patient may eagerly agree to come, but may not feel up to it at the very last moment. This reminds me of a friend's invitation to attend a men's church dinner. It was the perfect invitation, and my husband was excited for over a week in expectation. The day arrived. His friend would be picking him up around 6 p.m. Getting dressed, he suddenly became ill. With tears in his eyes, he realized he couldn't go.

Did his friend understand? Yes, he was our Christian physician.

Not everyone "understands." The word *cancer* sometimes brings unrealistic fears. Some acquaintances and friends behaved as if the cancer might be contagious. No—a handshake, a hug, or a pat on the back will *not* contaminate! Quite the opposite in fact; the touches and hugs are emotionally medicinal to both the giver and the receiver!

What we found most disconcerting was that some people erroneously believed that our conversational focus might be limited to the diagnosis. Would our intellect, interests, and hobbies be instantly dissected from our life? Would our brains be "re-wired"? No.

Fortunately, my husband's coworkers called him at home—and even at the hospital—for his opinion on computer problems. Rather than disturbing him, the calls affirmed him as a team member. These calls made him feel *needed*—the cancer was secondary to his knowledge.

With time, neighbors and friends came to the realization that we were still "us," so they relaxed. Patience is the key. As we learned, an illness affects far more people than the patient.

The third need is normalcy.

4

The Tollbooth

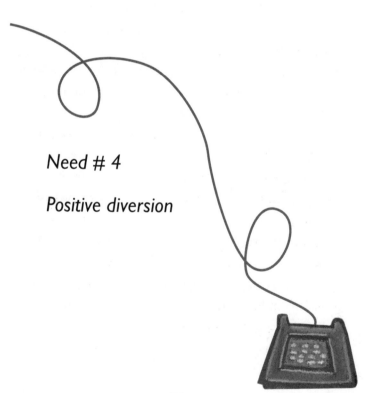

Need # 4

Positive diversion

Treatment. At this point on the "road to recovery," family and friends become vital. This period is the most challenging physically, mentally, and spiritually for the patient and family.

One enters the medical environment of unfamiliar surroundings, strange equipment, and odd smells. Almost within hours, an atypical working knowledge of tubing, mechanical beds, beeping equipment, and call buttons becomes typical.

Inconvenient schedules that continue around the clock now become life-saving and thus *convenient*. Ongoing treatment with synchronized chemotherapy becomes welcomed at any time, night or day. Hourly nursing assessments become comforting, yet the hours of the night become like the hours of the day. Any consecutive hours of sleep are priceless.

The hospital becomes a theoretical tollbooth on the highway of life. The toll is uncertain both financially and physically. Expenditures include parking fees, meal money, transportation, and medical and prescription bills. Physically, the toll to the patient and caregiver includes fatigue and anxiety.

Parking tokens make wonderful gifts. In many cases, cafeteria vouchers can be purchased for the family. Rather than sending flowers, evaluate the family's needs to determine the best use of your money.

This is the opportunity to "share batteries" as a friend or family member. Just as a cell phone must be recharged to be effective, so must a caregiver. This is an action opportunity to share your energy, strength, and vitality in allowing the caregiver time to "recharge." Volunteer to sit with the patient for a few hours or a day. What responsibilities could you—or a group—do to facilitate recharging time for the family?

Days in the hospital are like a monotonous highway in the desert. Diversions that provide a detour from this highway are greatly appreciated. *Short* calls or visits to the hospital, unexpected gifts with well wishes, and especially cards can brighten an entire day! Gifts or loans of inspirational and/or motivational books are as useful as a roadmap to a weary traveler. The messages read instill a renewal, both spiritually and mentally.

Most hospitals offer free use of a videocassette recorder or player if the patient requests one, so the gift or loan of videotapes is an excellent "recharge" and serves as a relaxing diversion. Choose tapes that are uplifting, motivational, and/or inspirational. Avoid any melancholy or disheartening themes.

Use your imagination in creating diversions. One midmorning, a friend stopped by the hospital with a large basket. Staying only a few minutes, he shared that he felt like we needed a picnic! Inside the basket were red-checkered paper napkins, homemade sandwiches, fancy cheeses, potato chips, and cookies. What is amazing is that we did feel like we were having a picnic!

One day we received a beautiful blue bouquet. Each and every patient on our hospital unit received one. The arrangement was formed from the most delicate, bright blue flowers and placed in a white wicker basket. It bore no card, but the nurse explained that it was from a former patient who sent the flowers each year to wish the current patients well. Humbly, this former patient asked to remain anonymous. He or she will never know what that kindness meant to us.

At the beginning of our hospitalizations, our family decided to pick a theme for each hospitalization and decorate the hospital room accordingly. Before each hospitalization, the family would go on a scavenger hunt—some decorations were bought, others borrowed. This became hilarious and therapeutic in anticipating the next hospital stay. One particular theme was Hawaiian, and the room included everything from coconuts to ukuleles!

Decorating the room brought laughter from the doctors, nurses, and other patients and their family members. It opened conversations that formed many close relationships during our stays.

In addition, we chose the most hilarious or brightest-colored nightwear. This, too, brought laughter and a sense of endearment.

Joy and laughter are rare commodities in treatment. Seek out avenues to share them and spread liberally. On Halloween, our young niece dressed up and filled a red arm basket with packets of microwave popcorn. She roamed the entire floor giving nurses, physicians, *anyone* that crossed her path, the gift of microwave popcorn. Within minutes, the sound of popping corn reverberated through the halls with the smell permeating the entire floor! Such little cost for so great a joy...

The fourth need is positive diversion.

5

Acceleration of Care

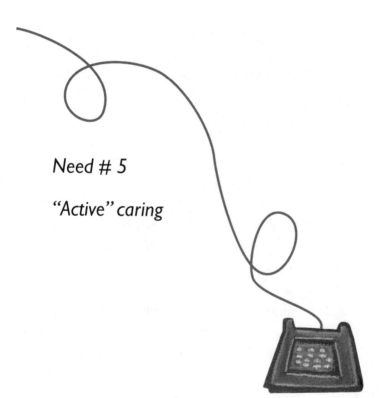

Need # 5

"Active" caring

One of the greatest lessons learned during this time was that the smallest act of kindness is worth more than a hundred people saying, "Call me if you need anything."

Don't ask. DO!

When a family member is in the hospital, the caretaker comes home from the hospital exhausted. One is too tired to cook, shop, or eat out. Worse still, the fatigue accumulates.

Visualize a fatigue that is almost paralyzing— emotionally and physically consuming—a relentless fatigue that hangs on like the flu.

Think carefully. What needed items would force you to go the grocery store after a long day at the hospital? What items would demand a detour from a hot bath and a recliner?

These are the items that you need to take to the family! Items such as toilet paper, clothes detergent, coffee, dishwashing detergent, etc. Think through your own purchase decisions. What items are vital or would be a treat?

My twin sister would specifically purchase grocery items that had been eliminated from our budget due to medical expenses. She'd return from the store with ice cream, cookies, snack foods, chips, etc. Her shopping trips felt as good as Christmas morning!

Some evenings, my sister would announce that it was "Pizza Night," or she'd declare—"I want Mexican food—let's go!" Of course, she knew I loved pizza and Mexican food, but she acted as if she wanted it!

This is the period when caring needs to be accelerated into action. Both men and women can effectively make a difference during this time. Small acts of kindness create not only opportunities for physical rest for the caregiver, but become emotionally therapeutic to both the giver and the receiver!

Ask the caregiver about specific needs that she/he may have—perhaps a repairman or exterminator is required, but no one is home to let them in. Volunteer to meet the need. If you have funds available and the need is great—pay the bill.

You may have to keep asking in order to help. Giving is easier than taking, and many people aren't used to asking or taking. Caregivers may be embarrassed to be in their situation. Some would go without before sharing a need. Be observant! Watch and listen for needs.

Pat's husband, in his fifties, was diagnosed with Alzheimer's. It became apparent that he couldn't work. From experience, I knew that obtaining disability benefits required time, and that money may be scarce. My sister and I went grocery shopping. As we delivered our purchases to the home, Pat's husband met us at the door. His immediate reaction was one of embarrassment, but my sister quickly said, "Would you do this for me if I had a need?"

He replied, "Oh yes, you know I would!"

That immediately restored his dignity; she was only doing what he would have willingly done for her. Humility, sincerity, and love will win trust.

The fifth need is "active" caring.

6

It's a Guy Thing

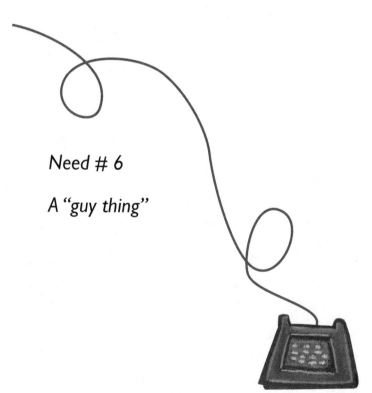

Need # 6

A "guy thing"

My husband was ill, and I was exhausted. A friend stopped by and remarked that the inspection sticker on my car was about to expire. I was just days away from the possibility of being ticketed! I never thought to look!

"It's a guy thing."

Some things guys are "just better at" when it comes to helping. Cars and yards are two of them.

Edging the yard was impossible. I found the edger heavy and difficult to keep steady. When I finished, the yard could be compared to a first grader's haircut by a classmate—gouges and scrapes all over! A gentleman neighbor "saw" the need and volunteered to take over the chore. (It took weeks for the yard to recover.)

Suggestions for guys helping during tragedy or sorrow include:

1. Check the car for state inspection deadlines and license expiration. Offer to take the car in for an inspection and to renew the license tags before the deadline.

2. Check under the hood for loose wires or hoses.
3. Check the oil and air filter, and replace if necessary.
4. Check the tires for wear, and advise if a tire change is needed. Air the tires if necessary.
5. Wash the car.
6. Fill the car up with gas.
7. Mow and edge the yard.
8. Assist in any needed repair; contact serviceman if needed.
9. Bring in trash cans each week.
10. Replace any burned-out light bulbs, especially exterior lights.
11. Keep an eye on the house during the vacancies.
12. Water plants, and trim any large broken limbs.
13. Give instructions as needed for simple scenarios, i.e., using a toilet plunger, flipping a breaker at the fuse box, etc.

I learned that changing light bulbs doesn't require a college education, but it does require strategy. Ten-foot ceilings and minute globe screws became my number one enemy. I felt defeated by a burned out light bulb.

My rearview mirror fell off the inside windshield of my car. A catastrophe! A neighbor, Buddy, seemed like Superman himself when he came to my rescue and repaired the mirror with a simple glue kit. In my panic I had envisioned a trip to the car dealership, a period of time without a car, and an expense I couldn't afford. His concern—and ten minutes of his time—not only removed a roadblock but also created a memory of kindness that will last a lifetime.

Simple repairs appear much larger to the inexperienced *and* especially when one is fatigued, apprehensive, and scared.

The sixth need is a "guy thing."

7

A Woman's Touch

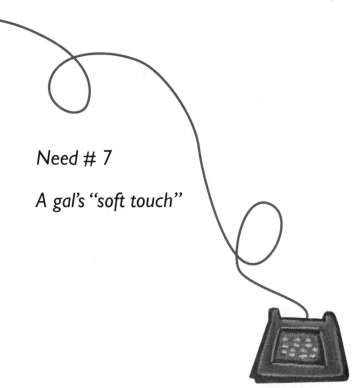

Need # 7

A gal's "soft touch"

Whether the patient is male or female, women seem to have a natural capacity for making difficult situations better. Whether it's a hot apple pie, a simple casserole, or a pot of coffee, her "soft touch" is always medicinal.

Possessing a special gift of intuitiveness, women seem to *know* when action is required. When to send a card, when to place that special note on the door, purchase that extra can of coffee, make the phone call, offer to pick up the kids. She just knows.

Ghada offered to shorten my husband's pajama pants to short-length, as Texas summers are hot. She took the leftover material and created hot pads as gifts for the family. These hot pads became treasured items, full of memories.

Debra created a huge basket full of crackers, granola bars, fruit rollups, and assorted snack foods to eat while we were in the hospital. Each choice from the basket was a treat and reminded us of her love and well-wishes.

Helen gave us a sandwich bag full of quarters. Why? Hospital vending machines serve as a vital food source twenty-four hours a day. She knew from her own experience that we would need coins—and she was correct.

Gal actions to help families in crisis include:

1. Volunteer to care for or transport children.
2. Give a box of stationery and/or thank-you cards with stamps.
3. Create novelty hats or scarves in the case of hair loss due to chemotherapy.
4. Volunteer to feed pets.
5. Water outside and/or inside plants.
6. Give the caretaker a few hours away by staying with the patient.
7. Give personal care items that smell wonderful (but be aware of the patient's allergies or reactions to perfumes).
8. Provide a picnic lunch in a basket that the family can share in the patient's room. It brightens a day!
9. Give colorful, novelty and/or flamboyant pajamas, bed throws, etc. (Hospitals are bland and gaiety is a rare commodity.)
10. Volunteer to provide transportation to the hospital or to other places if needed.

Marilyn brought over her banana nut bread. It was her tradition when one of her friends got the flu or other ailment. She always said it would "cure what ailed you," and the "love of the bread" always seemed to work. We accepted her gift as a welcomed sign.

The seventh need is a gal's "soft touch."

8

Taking Food
It Ain't Rocket Science

Need # 8

"Meal memories"

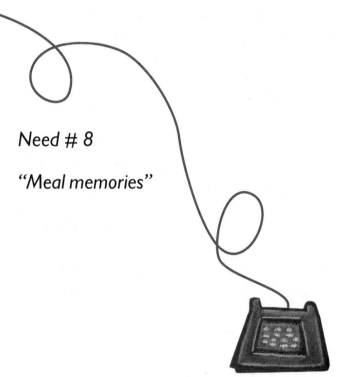

The gift of food is truly a chapter in itself. I have talked to several families who have gone through illnesses or tragedies, and I found similar experiences among them.

First, take all gifts of food in containers that don't have to be returned. Keeping track of dishes and finding time to return them is an additional responsibility the family doesn't need.

Second, never, ever, send a dish or plate that has been in the family for years. It happened to us. Attempting to share her very best, an older woman brought a cake on a family heirloom plate. Upon returning to pick up her dish from the church, she discovered it wasn't there. This created additional stress and anguish to both the giver and receiver. The dish was never found. Her sadness added to my sadness.

Choose a dish or menu that has been tried and tested. Never prepare a dish you've never prepared before.

Presentation is *key* in your gift of food. The appearance should say, "We care"; "You are special." It should entice the weary soul to eat. If your heart isn't in the gift, the gift will reflect it.

The most special "meal memory" we experienced was the gift of an entire ice chest of fresh gulf shrimp! Friends traveled hours to personally deliver it! Like Forrest Gump, for days we had fried shrimp, boiled shrimp, shrimp salad, shrimp fettuccini. We loved it!

If you face time constraints in cooking, provide a hoagie sandwich meal to be taken to the home or the hospital! Fancy bread, deli lunchmeat, sliced cheeses, pickles, chips, etc. A wonderful treat! This can be used multiple times and multiple ways by the family.

Many hospitals have specified refrigerators for inpatient use. Any leftover food can be labeled with the patient's name and refrigerated. This will reduce meal costs to the caregiver as well.

Don't take highly spiced food, but don't prepare under-seasoned dishes. Make your dish as you would at home.

Avoid dishes with gravy and vegetables, such as goulash—the appearance is unappetizing.

Desserts are enticing and will get the weariest caregiver to eat. Fatigue robs the appetite as well as the energy.

An idea to create laughs and lift spirits is to attach tags or labels to your dishes:

"Sweet-Like-*Suzie* Homemade Pie" using the patient's name

"Toasting You with a Roast!"

"Get-Well Chicken—It Will Have You Crowing!"

"Angel Eggs"

"You're-So-Nice-Rice"

"I've *Bean* Missing You!"

"Doctor Prescribed Chicken Soup"

"Recovery Ravioli"

Use your imagination and have fun. The patient and family will too! The gift of laughter is *priceless*. I use pinking shears and colored paper and place the tag on top of the foil. Small, cost-free extras can bring a lot of joy. If you are preparing food for one or two people, purchase colorful glass plates at the dollar store and prepare individual plates. The reuse of your gift plate will remind the patient and family of your good wishes.

It is important to find out from a family member how many people will be eating the meal that you are bringing. Many times, family members will be in town and helping out—especially on the weekends. You will want to take enough to feed everyone and once again assist the weary caregiver. Not having enough food creates additional stress.

Ask if the patient or family has any diet restrictions or personal dislikes. This shows sincerity and an honest desire to create a meal memory. Why take a meatloaf, when the patient has never *liked* meatloaf? It is just as easy to make something he or she likes. Ask the patient, "What would YOU like to have?" This simple question gives the patient CONTROL—something that many times he or she feels has been lost. The illness has necessitated so many decisions that are out of the patient's control.

Delivery of the food should be cheerful and encouraging. It should set the stage for your "meal memory." Make your visit brief, but loving.

An addition to your meal, once again, could be an inspirational book. Many times the patient is as hungry for spiritual food as for physical food.

The eighth need is for "meal memories."

9

Bunker Buddies
Staying "In" for the Battle

Need # 9

A buddy in your "bunker"

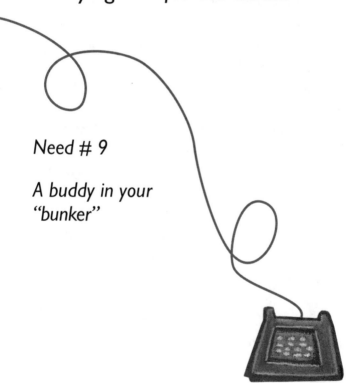

Treatment continues...tests are scheduled... and once again, the familiar waiting. The cycle seems to repeat endlessly. Days turn into weeks and weeks into months.

Like soldiers in battle, our family felt war-weary. We even looked different—like soldiers who had seen too much combat. The warring was so long that most of our friends returned home to their normal lives.

The cards and calls that once arrived frequently now slowed to a dribble or stopped. Only the "bunker buddies" remained. These I can number on one hand. Perhaps... a couple of fingers.

One of the bunker buddies was my brother-in-law David. Owning his own business, he found computer tasks that could keep my husband busy. It didn't matter if he wanted to work one hour or three hours. Almost every day, you could find David and my husband having lunch together at a local restaurant. In the evening and on weekends, they would be inseparable, sitting outside, fishing, or watching sports on television.

Bunker buddies are the friends who actively call, e-mail, send cards, encourage, and look for avenues in which to help. They listen to your conversation, dissecting the words, planning their next intervention.

Intervention? Yes—intervention.

Is the patient discouraged by recent test results? The bunker buddy calls office colleagues/friends/ church and asks that cards be sent. The response from the patient? A sense of encouragement and love—a renewal of hope! And, of course, they never knew the call was made.

One afternoon, the mail brought notification that our COBRA insurance had been cancelled—again! Having delivery confirmation of the payments, the insurance company errors were becoming overwhelming and time consuming. Disheartened by yet another challenge, my husband cried.

Within minutes, DeWayne, our Sunday school teacher, arrived—another bunker buddy who visited at least weekly. In the past, he too had used COBRA insurance. He explained that his policy had been cancelled six times in error! His empathy was sincere and comforting.

Birthday or anniversary? The bunker buddy takes action!

Is *the* ball game or golf match on television? The buddy is there beside you, rooting—even if it is for the other team or player! The buddy is there.

Dr. Ladage, one more bunker buddy, would routinely make house calls. After a brief exam, he frequently would settle in with my husband to watch a golf match on television. Each had his own favorite golfer and hopes of "his" golfer being the winner.

A bunker buddy is someone who will listen to your fears when the bullets are flying, and understand. Such friends give you courage. They are there until the battle is either won or lost. They are not in for a tour of duty; they signed up as career soldiers.

The ninth need is a buddy in your "bunker."

10

Fiction or Reality?
The Final Remaining Choices

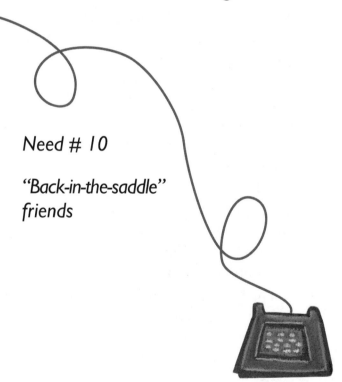

Need # 10

*"Back-in-the-saddle"
friends*

I t had to be fiction. A dream—no, a nightmare! It couldn't be reality...

My mind was frozen like a deep pond in the middle of winter. I couldn't even breathe. My chest felt so tight that I was sure that I would suffocate. No one seemed to be aware of the all-out panic that surged through my veins.

The hospital examination room, once a room of expectant opportunity, now felt like a jail cell. And justifiably so, as the doctor gently gave my husband, in essence, his death sentence.

Cancer had won.

It is human nature to expect "to win" in any battle or war. The defeat was as unexpected as a surprise espionage attack. Camouflaged, the enemy of cancer had been silently conquering.

The options, ultimately, were three. Two were experimental treatments with no promise of survival and debilitating side effects. The third was no intervention.

A few days later, Dr. Ladage kindly advised my

husband to "take option number three." In our case, the results would inevitably be the same. Had there been an option offering real hope for recovery, we would have taken it.

His honesty and insight gave my husband six wonderful months that included a trip to Cancun, fishing, golfing, and precious moments with friends, his children, and grandson. The trip to Cancun included the entire family and provided fun, laughter, and special shared memories for each family member.

Again, the greatest need and desire during this time was "normalcy." The diagnosis wasn't ignored or even denied. Our focus was simply "getting back to normal as much as possible"—leaving behind the "world of hospitalizations and treatment."

During this time, the acts of kindness that seemed to bring the greatest joy to my husband were the cards. Friends began sending cards telling him how much he meant to them, the acts of kindness he had shared, and special recollections together.

These personal notes were a gift—a priceless gift that shared how his life had impacted their own. He was amazed and humbled; many times he had forgotten the memories mentioned, and the notes brought those memories back to him. He grew to recognize more clearly that his life had purpose.

One young man wrote that Bill was like a father to him and that he wouldn't be where he is today without Bill. My husband never realized the impact he had on this young man's life until he received this card.

Friends would invite him to play a few holes of golf or go to lunch. His advice was sought for computer problems (his niche), and he rallied to the need. This, in turn, bolstered his morale as well. He felt "back in the saddle," and friends helped him "stay in the saddle" as long as possible.

Our Sunday school class brought food once a week, over our objections, because we really "didn't need it." We may not have needed it physically, but we *did* need it on every other level. Each dish represented love, compassion, and caring. A simple pot of beans conveyed a million dollars' worth of joy and served as a tangible sign of *"I'll be there for you."*

As my husband weakened, the invitations paralleled. Golf friends would come over to watch golf tournaments on television rather than asking him to *go* play golf.

As he continued to weaken, family members volunteered to stay by his side, allowing me some time to rest. It also provided their own special times together.

The tenth need is "back-in-the-saddle" friends.

11

The Final Farewell

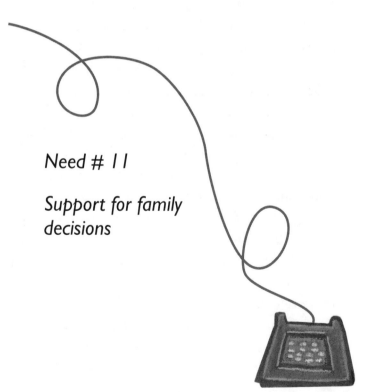

Need # 11

Support for family decisions

The final farewell came like unexpected snow. A beauty and a peace descended; the bedroom felt like a cathedral. The worst moment of my life became one of the most profound. I felt I was allowed to witness a secret rite of passage—a spiritual mystery. It was an awe-filled experience in which I felt the love of God envelop me with a supernatural serenity. I was now alone. After thirty-one years of marriage, I was scared.

I was also fatigued with a tiredness that I had never known. Even my bones ached with tiredness. My goal had been to take care of my husband at home, and I felt a victory in succeeding.

I felt like a marathon runner who collapses upon crossing the finishing line. Exhaustion enveloped my body like a python, squeezing me limp in its grip. Weariness made my immediate responsibilities seem overwhelming.

The funeral was purposely planned to be small. After months of being rendered powerless by an insidious disease, the funeral was one of the first things I *could* control. I wanted it intimate. Some "friends" voiced disappointment that the funeral was conducted soon after the death. They complained that the funeral should have been postponed to allow former employees and friends from far-away to attend, but the funeral decisions, I believe, had been "earned" by the immediate family. In reality, the family didn't have the strength mentally or physically to postpone it several days. Assistance would have been required for travel instructions, motel, and meals. Some friends understood, but others did not.

In lieu of flowers, I asked that people make donations to the charity of the giver's choice in my husband's memory. Some found the lack of flowers disheartening. In reality, hundreds of dollars were given to churches and charities.

Charitable donations serve as a tangible continuation of the loved one's memory. The family receives word of the contribution two to four weeks later, making your gift very special. Some families do find comfort in the presence of flowers during the visitation and funeral. Follow the cues given in the obituary or in comments you have heard the loved ones make in the past.

By now, friends and family have, for the most part, moved on. During this time, the reality of the loss is painfully clear, and your memorial gift has a healing power.

Rather than spending a large amount of money on the funeral, I chose a graveside memorial service. Others have the opinion that the amount of money spent on a funeral reflects the depth of one's love. Opinions are as varied as individuals. Ultimately, the choice is the family's to make. The first gift you can give as a friend is to support the family in their decisions.

The second immediate need is food brought to the home. Meat and cheese trays are practical and can be used for sandwiches in subsequent meals. Fruit trays are a treat as well. A suggestion would be to take two casseroles—one ready to eat and one to freeze. This will serve as a dinner resource after everyone leaves! Your kindness will be doubly enjoyed!

Appreciated practical items to bring include paper plates, plastic silverware, napkins, plastic foam cups, coffee, and canned drinks. This provides the tableware to serve the family and guests, while allowing easy cleanup.

> *The eleventh need is support for family decisions.*

12

A Life Recruiter

Need # 12

A "life recruiter"

As a friend, you can become a "life recruiter." Just as a military recruiter wants you to join his branch of service, you can encourage the bereaved to join "life" again. It's human nature to retreat when hurt. It will take your love and encouragement for them to "re-enlist."

The first year is the hardest. It is a year of change, adjustment, and sadness. Cards, cheery phone calls, and invitations can make a great difference in the length and the severity of the bereavement. Each card or phone call is therapeutic. Remember that your life busily moves on, but for the grieving the world has temporarily stopped.

In the first few months, my brother-in-law planted a memorial flowerbed with a sign that read, "Bill's Memorial Garden." An angel birdbath became the focal point, with several angelic posed sculptures placed strategically throughout the flowers and ivy. It was a positive healing action for the entire family.

The first anniversary is the hardest—especially when no one remembers.

Mark the date of the death on the calendar and send a card a year later to the family.

During the first year, the spouse and family members look back as if gazing into the rearview mirror. One reminisces, "Last year at this time, we..." Going into the second year is like putting a blank sheet of paper between the chapters of your life. It forces one to look ahead through the windshield of life.

Gifts of books about bereavement can become survival textbooks—giving reassurance that what they are going through is "normal." (It doesn't *feel* normal...) But bereavement is unique to each individual, so be attuned to the grieving person's needs. Active caring is needed again to assist in the grieving process. Provide invitations *and* transportation to events. Call and say, "I'm picking you up at five—dress casual." Invite yourself over for coffee or say, "I'm bringing supper, and we can eat on your front porch—see you at six!" Use your imagination! But be sensitive to the individual. Be willing to take "no" for an answer. Keep your eyes and ears open to creative ways you can recruit your friend back to normal life.

The twelfth need is a "life recruiter."

13

"I Don't Know What to Do!" Guide

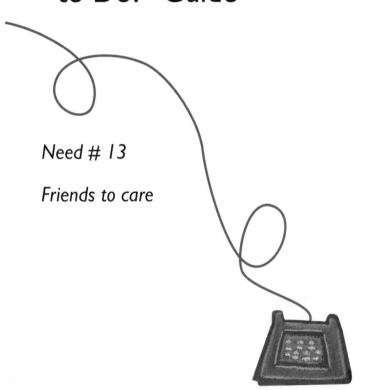

Need # 13

Friends to care

Here are a few things you can do that are sure to be appreciated by a patient and/or a patient's family:

1. Place a blooming plant by the front door so it will be found upon returning from the hospital.
2. Place a note of encouragement on the door.
3. Pick the newspaper from the yard, and place it by the door.
4. Put a "welcome home" yard sign in front of the home upon discharge(s) from the hospital.
5. Give a box of stationery and/or thank-you cards with stamps.
6. Give or loan inspirational books and upbeat movie videos.
7. Give the family toilet paper, coffee, casseroles, snacks, and cleaning items such as detergent, dishwashing soap, etc.
8. Purchase hospital parking tokens for the family, or give parking money.
9. Volunteer to feed pets or to let them out during the day.

10. Volunteer to care for or transport children.
11. Notify family that a pizza is on the way. (Call and order delivery upon their return from the hospital.)
12. Send greeting cards to the home rather than the hospital—mail is received more quickly and serves as a treat twice! The card comes once to the home and is enjoyed a second time when taken to the hospital! If you do send mail to the hospital, put the patient's address as the return address. If the patient has been discharged, it will be "returned" to the patient's home!
13. Give holiday decorations for appropriate holidays. (This brightens the room and provides a sense of normalcy.)
14. Volunteer transportation to the hospital or elsewhere if needed.
15. Give blood if needed and if you are able to do so.
16. Give motivational posters for the room.
17. Give the family a calendar to post treatment and appointments.
18. Give a nice room deodorizer—hospitals don't smell "homey."
19. If it is a long hospital stay, send plants rather than flowers. (Dying flowers are depressing.)

20. Start a prayer chain, and make the family aware of the prayers.
21. Put the Christmas tree up and/or take it down.
22. Bring a "welcome home cake" upon a discharge.
23. Schedule a massage, manicure, or pedicure for the caregiver or patient.
24. Give a gift certificate at a beauty shop for the caregiver or patient.
25. A headset and CDs make a great gift or loan while in the hospital.
26. Give a guest book to record their visitors.
27. Give a small book in which the family can write frequently called phone numbers. (Make sure it is small enough that the family can carry it with them.)
28. Give a journal for note making and physician instructions.
29. Water houseplants and/or outside plants.
30. Volunteer to clean the house.
31. Give a small bell for the patient to ring for assistance at home.
32. Give a miniature foghorn for the patient to use in case of emergency when family members are outside.
33. Give a magazine subscription.
34. Offer to collect the mail each day.

35. Offer to loan a wheelchair or any medical items you may have.
36. Give a computer game or software program.
37. Give simple gifts such as drinking straws, a drinking cup with a lid, or socks.
38. If the family is staying in a hotel or hospitality facility, pay for one night or longer.
39. Sweat suits are practical and comfortable gifts for both men and women.
40. Small bouquets taken often are more appreciated that a one-time larger bouquet.
41. Give colorful and hilarious boxer shorts for men.
42. Give attractive nightgowns that can be worn without a robe.
43. Give small sized toiletry items for the hospital stay(s).
44. Give his/her favorite candy or bakery treat.
45. Give a bed tray or a TV tray.

Don't Give

1. Sports equipment or sports paraphernalia if the prognosis is uncertain. This creates a sense of loss not only for the receiver, but the family as well.
2. Medical reading material of a negative nature; every case is different.

3. Movies, books, magazines, or articles that are disheartening or contain discouraging/melancholy messages or plots.

4. Liquor—most medications cannot be mixed with alcohol.

5. Heavily scented colognes, lotions, or toiletries.

6. See-through sleep attire inappropriate for hospital use.

7. Electrical decorations for the hospital room, such as miniature Christmas trees, strand lights, and so on. Hospital fire codes won't allow usage.

8. Cigarettes.

9. Invitations to long-lasting events that would tire the patient.

10. Long telephone calls or personal visits.

The thirteenth and overall need is for friends to care.

14

Bee Statements

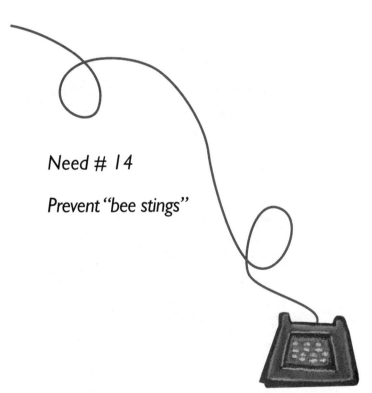

Need # 14

Prevent "bee stings"

Many times in an effort to encourage or console, we make "bee statements." These are genuine, heartfelt statements that sound as practical and nonthreatening as a honeybee, yet the words sting the heart of the receiver.

"He is in a better place."

This is true, but the reality is that the loss is painful and given the choice, the family would prefer the family member with them.

"He'll be better off."

Once again true, but the grieving family feels that "better off" would be a normal life together.

"God needed another angel in heaven."

Don't put the blame on God.

"It was just his (or her) time to go."

Another way to put the blame on God.

"Do you miss him?"

Sincere, but self-evident.

"Do you wish it was you instead?"

Inadvertently introduces guilt.

"If you think it hurts to lose a spouse, wait until you lose a child..."

This devalues the loss.

"You wouldn't want him to suffer..."

Another alternative would be recovery.

"Are you going to stay in the house?"

Are you house hunting?

"Do you think you'll remarry?"

Devalues the loss.

"Are you going to sell the boat?"

Bargain shopping?

"What size shoes did he wear?"

Yes, the question was asked.

Don't ask about the possessions of the deceased. Let the family make decisions on their own. The "bee statements" or questions in this arena appear to the bereaved as an avenue of self profit.

"He died quick!"

For the family, the months didn't seem "quick."

"You'll have to get your mind busy on other things."

Insensitive.

> *The fourteenth need is "to prevent bee stings"?*

15

Butterfly Words

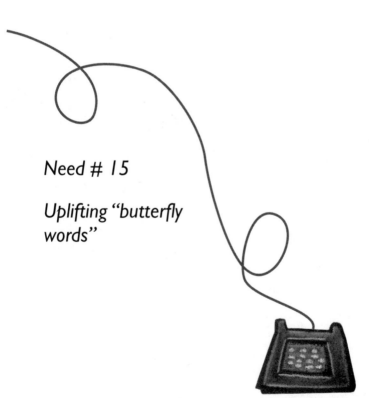

Need # 15

Uplifting "butterfly words"

A metamorphosis occurs in a loss. As surely as a caterpillar never expected to lose its cocoon, become a butterfly and fly, the grieving person never expected the loss. Now, life as they know it will never be the same. "Normal" will never be... normal again.

As if emerging from a cocoon, the still-moist "wings" of the grieving feel strange. It is a time of adjustment and need for protection. Yet decisions have to be made, and quickly.

Like an updraft breeze to a butterfly, your words need to lift the heart of those grieving. It isn't a time of questioning; it is a time of comforting.

Don't be philosophical and ask questions, suggesting if alternate treatment was tried or if "that" physician was used. This conveys that mistakes on the part of the bereaved in some way contributed to the death.

Sometimes you simply don't know what to say. Just be honest. Tell the family, "I don't know what to say." Your calling or coming over says more than any eloquent words or phrases. Presence has more power than words. A hug says volumes. The family needs presence, not precepts.

The best statement to make—the statement that is most comforting is, "I want you to know that I am praying for you." And *do* pray.

Comforting to the family are positive stories or incidents that include their loved one. Sharing these memories provides consolation to the family that the loved one won't be forgotten and reminds them that this life touched many other lives.

At this time and as additional time passes, remind family members how proud their dad/mother/etc. would be of them—of their accomplishments and/or positive role in life. This is medicinal to the heart of the grieving.

With children especially, continue telling stories about their deceased parent. Give them added memories that their young minds can hold onto and be proud of. Help them remember the deceased even if they were too young at the time of the death to really be able to remember.

Last, be patient and willing to listen. As it does for an emerging butterfly, the future feels different and frightening for the bereaved. The "normal" life as a caterpillar is forever over.

The fifteenth need is uplifting "butterfly words."

16

Holidays
No Ho-Ho-Ho

Need # 16

Sensitivity on holidays

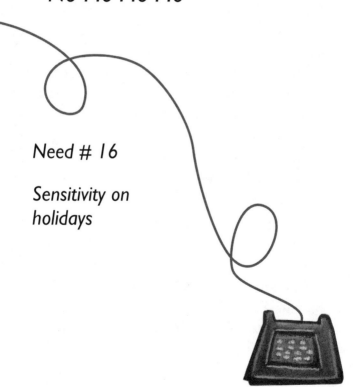

Holidays are the worst...any holiday, but especially Christmas. A person who is grieving can be moving forward, looking through the "windshield of life," and a holiday will put on the brakes.

Holidays force one to look into the "rearview mirror."

Reminders are everywhere: store decorations, music, traditional church and community programs, wassail at the bank...Even the smell of a fresh Christmas tree in a store lot brings tears.

Remember the year that...

Valentine's Day—No flowers or that "gushy card."

Birthday. No dinner out together. Birthdays serve as a reminder that you aren't going to grow old together. Around birthdays, I found myself noticing older couples, walking hand-in-hand, gray-haired and slightly bent. They didn't seem to notice that they'd grown old—still in love. The sweetness brought tears—tears of joy for them, and what could have been.

Add to this, feeling responsible for keeping the holidays "happy" and not appearing melancholy around friends and family members.

It's like being a guest and having to eat liver and pretend that you like it...

The first year of holidays after someone you love dies is the most difficult. The memories of the last such holiday are fresh, with emotions easily recaptured.

My friend Bettye worked as a registered nurse. For years, on Valentine's Day, her husband sent roses. It was his traditional act of love. On the first Valentine's Day following his death, she reported to the hospital as usual for her shift in the emergency room. Upon entering the hospital, she saw dozens of roses that had been delivered to employees and patients. She excused herself and let the tears fall.

An insensitive coworker, believing she was upset because she didn't get flowers, said, "Here! If you're that upset about a flower, take one of mine!"

Family members, friends, and coworkers should be extra sensitive during the holidays. Send a card and be honest:

"This must be a difficult time for you—I am praying for you."

"Thanksgiving is a time of year that we remember what we have to be grateful for—I'm grateful to have known (the name of the deceased)."

"Easter is a time for renewal and, I know, a time of renewal in your own life."

"Valentine's Day is a day of love. Please know that I love you as a friend."

When inviting a person in grief for the holidays, be aware that he or she may not feel like coming. Remember: "Don't invite—HIKE!" Go get him or her! Your sincere invitation will draw the person out. But if the bereaved person remains insistent about not going, do not be offended.

During the holidays, call and say, "I've volunteered you to help…" My sister volunteered me to help decorate the church for Christmas. How could I say no? She had already volunteered me! When I arrived, the church was buzzing with activity and laughter. It was contagious! In minutes, I was in the spirit! Again, though, do not feel hurt if the person gives an insistent "no" to your suggestion. Personally, I found Christmas trips therapeutic. On a particular trip to Mexico, our family wrapped gifts for children in decorative paper—red for boys and green for girls.

On Christmas morning, we asked hotel employees about their children. Upon learning the gender of the children, we gave them the appropriate gifts to take home. I will never forget their surprise and delight at the unexpected gifts. It also created new memories for me!

You can become a part of new holiday memory making! It requires so little...

The sixteenth need is sensitivity on holidays.

17

To Care or
Not to Care

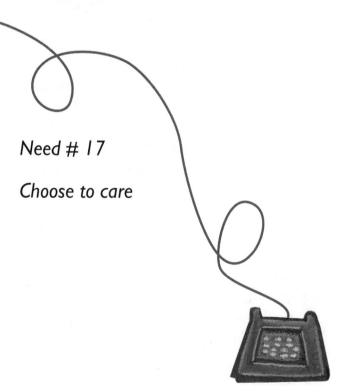

Need # 17

Choose to care

I am convinced that a person can face the most challenging situation positively and courageously if he or she believes someone cares.

As a friend or family member, you have that power to make the difference. It will require selflessness, patience, and understanding. At times, it will require you to go the extra mile.

After the funeral, I looked as exhausted as I felt. My bright blue eyes were surrounded by large dark circles. My sister announced, "Tomorrow we're going for a facial and massage!" The experience was as if Jesus himself were there—loving and caring. I felt overwhelmed. It was a day I will never forget until I myself am laid to rest. It was a gift of love and physical renewal.

Acts of kindness during a difficult time are magnified in the minds and hearts of the receiver. Never underestimate a simple idea that you have to help. God will use it—do it!

The smallest executed act means more than the largest intent. For example, a gift of pinto beans and cornbread is appreciated more than a steak dinner that was never delivered.

An older widow, living solely on Social Security, brought just that—pinto beans and cornbread. Because of her advanced age and meager income, her gift meant more to me than any other dish brought. She taught me a valuable lesson—that God can use anyone, in any situation, to share love.

You have the opportunity to etch God's love upon the hearts of family members, friends, acquaintances, and yes, even strangers.

Look around your church or neighborhood. Who is in need of God's kindness? I promise you won't have to look very long.

Remember: Don't ask—DO!

The ultimate need is for you to choose to care.

18

Down the Road

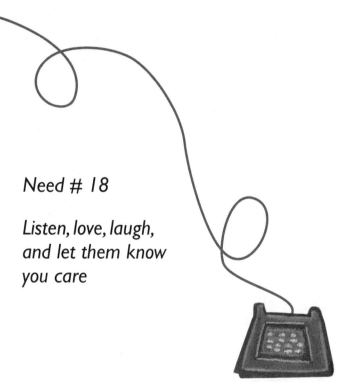

Need # 18

Listen, love, laugh, and let them know you care

It's been two and a half years. How can time pass so slowly and yet so fast? A paradox that teases the mind and the heart. A time to reflect and project.

One of the lessons quickly learned is that being a widow is more expensive. The chores once on the "honey-do list" now require payment. In my first summer as a widow, I experienced the following:

- The lawnmower had a flat tire.
- My back doorknob refused to lock.
- The kitchen ceiling fan began making a "roaring" sound.
- Wasps formed a nest in my garage; I am allergic to stings.
- The hot water heater needed to be adjusted.
- The kitchen faucet leaked.
- A storm toppled a huge tree, blanketing the ground with limbs and debris.
- The swinging gate on my picket fence refused to swing.
- The refrigerator made noises.

- My computer got a virus.
- A six-foot rattlesnake stretched out to sun in my backyard.

There was no "honey" for the "honey-do list."

Second lesson learned. Family cannot always be available to assist with immediate needs, but neighbors and friends may fill the gap.

My two children lived hours away with my son's employment requiring overtime and emergency on-call status. In addition, they had responsibilities with their children and church activities.

In July, a violent and unexpected storm struck. Within minutes, the hundred-year-old tree that graced my country backyard with shade and beauty…fell. *Fell* isn't the correct word. It was torn, ripped, mangled, and left with awkwardly hanging branches—limbs hanging like broken legs bent the wrong way. It was as if, the storm itself wanted to leave a monument demonstrating its power. Lawn equipment and furniture were blown across the road; hanging flower baskets were ripped away, with the hooks bent straight! Bedded plants were pulled from the ground, leaving gaping holes as the only sign of their previous existence. I stared at the scene of devastation with disbelief. Tears welled in my eyes, and I wondered, "where do I begin?"

Within minutes, neighbors and friends descended with chainsaws and limb cutters. Hours passed, and a burn pile rose toward the sky. It was determined that a tractor would be required to haul away the trunk pieces. A few days later, I awoke to the sound of machinery—it was Don and Tommy, two brothers who lived down the road. Tommy was directing his brother as he maneuvered his green-and-yellow John Deere tractor. Each massive piece had to be carefully "forked" to safely remove, or it would roll off dangerously. My yard was restored from the havoc of the storm.

This unexpected gift from my neighbors was *priceless*.

Another blessing! My nephew Brandon called. He asked me to prepare a "need to do list" and said that he would be in town the following Saturday. As promised, he was at my door wearing workclothes and a tool belt around his waist. It was quickly obvious that the day was MINE! I was giddy with excitement! He systematically attacked my list of current needs one-by-one. Many repairs required only minutes and simple tools.

His "love gift" required no money, only the precious gift of time and talent. Refusing any compensation, he left my home in top working order!

Third lesson learned. Some friends want to "help you" in the grieving process by "introducing you to someone."

It's like getting a new puppy when your dog dies. Although well intended, such an act introduces guilt. After nearly thirty-two years of marriage, I still *felt married!* I needed to go through the grief process *alone*. I needed time to heal. A death of a spouse is like pulling two boards apart that have been glued together. With a split, there is damage.

Allow widows or widowers time. They will indicate when they are ready for a "friend." Don't assume to *know* when the timing is right.

Fourth lesson learned. People hold a misconception that once the spouse or family member dies the tragedy is over and the family returns to normalcy.

False. The family is *never* the same. Many times, friends and even the church "move on," missing opportunities to minister.

Fifth lesson learned. Now alone, one feels out of the mainstream.

Sitting in church alone is...lonely. You are no longer in the familiar "couples class" in Sunday school. I found the thought of going to the "singles class" unimaginable—I was married last week—last year! "Single"—the word sounded so lonely.

After a death, conscientious efforts need to be made to reintegrate the widow/widower into an appropriate Sunday school class. Be cognizant of those sitting alone in church. Make it a personal ministry to seek out those persons and sit by them. Just one word of encouragement can brighten an entire day!

Sixth lesson learned. It *does* "get better with time," but you find that simple, inconsequential triggers hurl you down "memory lane" and into tears.

A song on the radio, a favorite plant you find blooming, finding a forgotten memento, and so forth turn on the weeping faucet. Becoming a widow/widower is like transplanting a fruit tree. One expects the tree to go into shock for a period of time before it begins growth again. *Nurturing* is the key for healthy survival and subsequent fruit production.

Seventh lesson learned. Weekends and holidays are more difficult.

Historically these are the days on which quality time was shared and the majority of memories made.

Eighth lesson learned. A pet serves as a valuable tool in the recovery process.

I found that my small dog provided comfort, companionship, security at night, and unconditional love. Somehow, having the dog, I didn't feel "alone."

Ninth lesson learned. A card or phone call is medicinal—literally.

Proverbs 16:24 (NIV) says, "Pleasant words are a honeycomb, sweet to the soul and healing to the bones." No truer words. A simple "thinking of you" card can be read, reread, and reread, ministering over and over, serving to heal physically and mentally.

Tenth lesson learned. People are drawn to you in their times of trouble.

The challenges you faced now become tools with which to help others. You know how to listen and when to or not to respond. You instinctively understand the keys in ministering:

> *The continuing need is for listening, love, laughter, and letting them know you care.*